CONTENTS

THE EARLY GREEKS

The first great civilization on mainland Greece began in about 2000 BC when groups of herdsmen left central Europe to settle further south. By about 1600 BC, these early Greeks, known as Mycenaeans, were at the height of their power. Heavily influenced by an older civilization on nearby Crete, they had built cities and palaces, set up trading links with neighbouring countries and learnt to write.

But the power and prosperity of the Mycenaeans did not last. Around 1200 BC, their civilization came to a mysterious end, and Greece entered a period of decline, known as the Dark Ages, during which the art of writing was lost.

A NEW BEGINNING

When the Dark Ages eventually ended in about 800 BC, Greek civilization began to emerge once more. Writing was rediscovered and the arts started to flourish. Overseas trading improved and lots of Greek colonies were set up around the Mediterranean and Black seas.

CLASSICAL GREECE

The years between 500 BC and the late 300s BC saw some of the greatest cultural advances of all. During this time, known as the Classical Period, famous temples were built and brilliant scholars, writers and artists were at work. Much of this book is written about that time.

The book also concentrates on life in Athens, because this is where most of our knowledge about the ancient Greeks comes from.

Many of the places mentioned in this book are shown on the map of ancient Greece opposite. The smaller map below shows the position of Greece in the world.

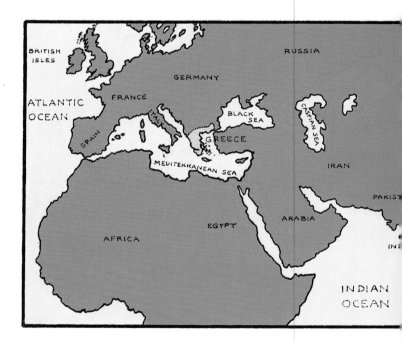

SCATTERED STATES

Greece is a country divided up by rugged mountains and deep valleys. In ancient times, these natural barriers made central government difficult and so lots of small, independent states grew up, each with its own city, farmland, villages, coins and laws. As the Greeks liked living in small communities, this system suited them well.

GREEKS

FACTS • THINGS TO MAKE • ACTIVITIES

RACHEL WRIGHT

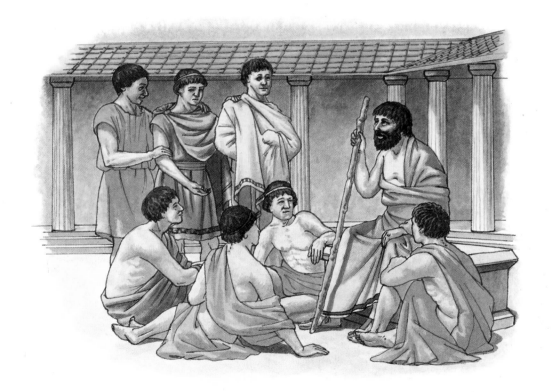

FRANKLIN WATTS
LONDON•SYDNEY

This edition 2008

Franklin Watts
338 Euston Road
London, NW1 3BH

Franklin Watts Australia
Level 17/207 Kent Street
Sydney, NSW 2000

© 1992 Franklin Watts

Editor: Hazel Poole
Consultant: Ann Pearson
Design: Sally Boothroyd
Photography: Chris Fairclough
Artwork: James Field, Mike Taylor

A CIP catalogue record for this book is available from
the British Library.

ISBN: 978 0 7496 7825 8
Dewey number: 938

Printed in Dubai

Franklin Watts is a division of Hachette Children's
Books, an Hachette Livre UK company.

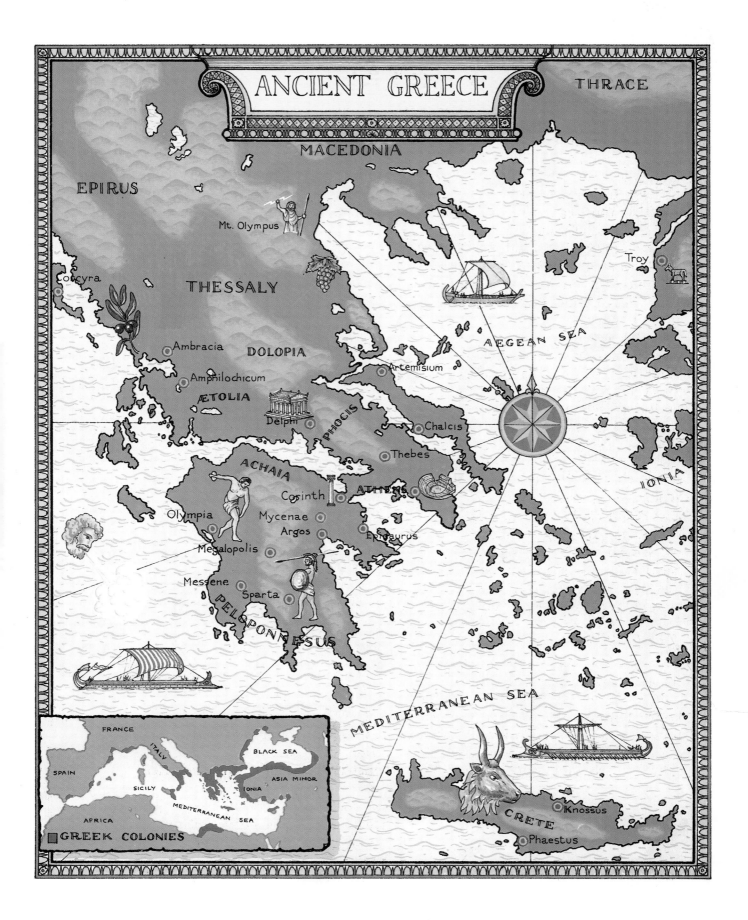

ANCIENT GREECE

THRACE

MACEDONIA

EPIRUS

Mt. Olympus

Troy

THESSALY

AEGEAN SEA

Corcyra

Ambracia

DOLOPIA

Amphilochicum

ÆTOLIA

Artemisium

Delphi

PHOCIS

Chalcis

Thebes

ACHAIA

Corinth

ATHENS

Olympia

Mycenae

Argos

Epidaurus

Megalopolis

Messene

Sparta

PELOPONNESUS

IONIA

MEDITERRANEAN SEA

CRETE

Knossus

Phaestus

FRANCE

ITALY

BLACK SEA

SPAIN

ASIA MINOR

SICILY

IONIA

MEDITERRANEAN SEA

AFRICA

GREEK COLONIES

PEOPLE POWER

At first, most Greek states were ruled by kings, groups of rich landowners or tyrants. But, by the beginning of the Classical Period, some states were using a system of government called democracy. Democracy gave all citizens the right to govern their state themselves. Women, foreigners and slaves, however, were not regarded as citizens and so they did not have a vote.

ATHENIAN DEMOCRACY

Athens was one of the first states to have a democracy. All Athenian citizens were expected to attend regular meetings to discuss public matters. The policies they debated and voted on were drawn up by a council of 500 men, who were chosen by "lot" each year. This was very much like picking names out of a hat.

Most government officials were chosen by lot. This meant that even the poorest citizen could find himself serving a term as a councillor or judge. The only officials not chosen by lot were the ten commanders of the army and navy. These military men were elected, and sometimes re-elected, each year. When war threatened, which in ancient times happened often, they had to lead their fellow citizens into battle.

MODERN DEMOCRACIES

Like ancient Greece, many modern countries have chosen democratic governments. However, because our countries are much bigger than the Greek states of old, politicians are elected to debate and vote on our behalf.

FARMERS AND CRAFTSMEN

The ancient Greek citizen liked to be his own boss, and many ran their own farm. The main crops grown were wheat and barley. However, because the rocky landscape and dry climate made good farmland scarce, farmers also cultivated grapes and olives which grew well on poor soil and mountainsides. The grapes were used to make wine, and the olives were pressed to produce oil for cooking, lamp fuel and soap.

Many townspeople earned their living as craftsmen. Craft workshops were small family businesses, run from home. Skills, such as pottery making, sculpting, metal working and carpentry, were probably passed from father to son.

◀ *This vase, made during the 300s BC, shows olive pickers at work. Greek pottery was often painted with scenes from daily life or stories of the gods.*

POTS AND POTTERS

The Greeks stored everything, from grain to perfume, in clay pots and bottles. These vessels were often beautifully decorated.

First, a design was painted on the pot with black slip. Then the pot was fired in a kiln. When the temperature reached about 800°C, the kiln's chimney was sealed. This reduced the amount of oxygen in the kiln and turned the whole pot black. When the chimney was re-opened, fresh oxygen rushed into the kiln and turned the unpainted parts of the pot red. The rest stayed black. Without thermometers, which hadn't yet been invented, this process must have taken ages to get right.

MAKE A GRECIAN VASE

Ask a grown-up to help you as the craft knife will be sharp!

You will need: a smooth-sided bottle • terracotta air-hardening modelling clay • rolling pin • modelling tool • damp sponge • craft knife • scissors • thick card • black acrylic paint • a wooden board to work on.

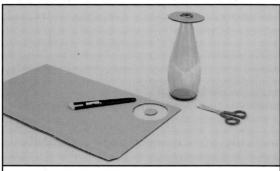

▲ **1.** Cut out a small circle of thick card and make a hole in its centre, just big enough to fit onto the neck of the bottle.

2. Roll out a sheet of clay of even thickness, large enough to cover the bottle and cardboard ring.

▲ **3.** Wrap the clay around the bottle and ring, and trim it so that all the edges just overlap. Smooth the joins and the rest of the vase with a damp sponge or wet fingers. If you find it easier, smooth the joins with a wooden modelling tool.
  Cut away any clay covering the bottle's opening, and leave the bottle somewhere warm to dry.

4. To make the handles, roll two "sausages" of clay. Lay your vase on its side, and smooth the ends of each handle into place. You'll need to put something under each handle to support them. Leave these supports in place while the handles dry.

5. When your vase has dried, paint a design on it, or paint the whole vase black, wait for the paint to dry, and then carefully scratch a design on it using the craft knife.

SECOND-CLASS CITIZENS

SLAVE-LABOUR

One of the reasons why many Greeks were able to run businesses and carry out public duties was because they owned slaves. Athens, like many other states, had a huge slave population. This was made up of prisoners of war and foreigners who had been bought by slave traders and then sold at auctions.

Household slaves who worked for kind owners were treated well, but those who worked in the silver mines suffered horribly. Branded and chained together, these wretched men spent most of their lives trapped in hot, narrow tunnels.

WIVES AND MOTHERS

In many ways, wealthy Greek women were not much better off than their slaves. They couldn't vote or own property, and they had to do what their male relatives told them. Rich wives spent most of their time at home, looking after their children and supervising household chores. If they wanted to go out, they had to be accompanied by a slave.

Women from poor families were less restricted. They had to do their own housework, which included collecting water from public fountains. Carrying heavy water pots can't have been fun, but at least it gave these women the chance to get out and about unchaperoned.

At Home with the Greeks

Most city dwellers lived in houses made of sun-dried mud bricks with wooden stairs, shutters and balconies. Although these mud bricks were cheap and easy to use, they were also rather soft. This was a great help to burglars. Instead of picking locks or squeezing through windows, they could simply break their way into a house by cutting through its walls!

Many houses were built around an open-air courtyard, in the middle of which stood an altar for family prayers. Wealthy households sometimes had a fountain in the courtyard as well, to supply them with water.

Most rooms opened inwards to the courtyard, rather than out on to the noisy, smelly street. Their glassless windows were small, to keep out the summer heat and winter cold.

LIVING APART

In every house, men and women had their own separate quarters. The men used their private room for entertaining guests. There they lounged on couches and ate their food off low three-legged tables.

The women used their quarters mostly for spinning, weaving and chatting with friends. They also spent a lot of time in the kitchen, baking bread in a pottery oven and cooking fish and vegetables over a charcoal fire. With only a hole in the roof to let out the smoke, the kitchen must have been like a sauna at times.

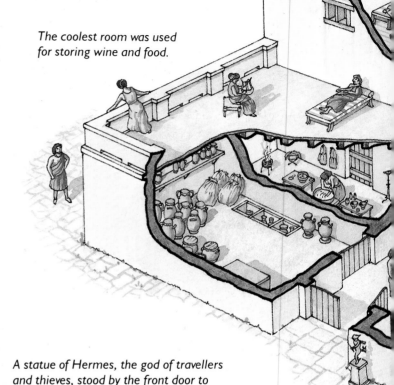

The coolest room was used for storing wine and food.

A statue of Hermes, the god of travellers and thieves, stood by the front door to protect the household.

SKIN SCRAPING

Few houses had a bath, so most people washed in a large pot instead. They rubbed olive oil into their skin, scraped it off with a curved bronze scraper, and then splashed themselves with water.

FIXTURES AND FITTINGS

Apart from couches, which also served as beds, the Greeks had chests for storing their clothes and baskets for keeping jewellery in. Other items, such as musical instruments and drinking cups, hung from pegs on the walls. The walls were sometimes decorated with colourful cloth, too, which was woven by the women of the house.

The roof was made of clay tiles.

The ground floor was made of earth or stone.

Although wealthy Greeks had chairs, most people sat on stools. At night, their rooms were lit by pottery lamps filled with olive oil, and in winter the rooms were heated by charcoal braziers. The combination of these burning fuels must have made the whole house incredibly smoky.

A craftsman often used a room at the front of his house as a workshop. Sometimes front rooms were rented out as a shop.

GODS AND GODDESSES

Like other ancient civilizations, the Greeks worshipped many different gods and goddesses.

Zeus was the king of gods and of men. The Greeks believed that when he threw his spear, lightning flashed and thunder roared.

Zeus's brother, Poseidon, ruled the sea. When angry, he would churn the sea into tidal waves or shake the Earth violently. Not surprisingly, sailors tried to keep Poseidon on their side by offering sacrifices to him.

Hera was Zeus's sister and wife. Worshipped as the goddess of marriage, she spent most of her time arguing with her husband about his love affairs!

Zeus's son, Apollo, was the god of the Sun, music and medicine.

Athena was the goddess of wisdom and warfare. She was also the patron goddess of Athens and a number of other Greek cities.

Athena was born in an unusual way. One day Zeus asked Hephaestos, the god of fire, to hit him on the head! Hephaestos obliged and Athena popped out of Zeus's head, fully armed!

Aphrodite was the goddess of love and beauty. Her winged son, Eros, made people fall in love by firing arrows into their hearts.

THE OLYMPIANS

Zeus, Poseidon, Hera, Aphrodite, Athena, Apollo and Hephaestos were part of a family of 12 gods known as the Olympians. These 12, who were the most powerful gods of all, were said to live on a cloud-covered mountain in Thessaly called Mount Olympus.

The Olympians were worshipped throughout Greece, but each state had its own local gods and goddesses as well. Many of these minor immortals were thought to live in caves, woods and streams.

HOLY HOMES

In public, the gods were worshipped outside magnificent temples made of limestone or marble. These temples were believed to be the earthly homes of the gods. When someone wanted to ask for heavenly help, they would go to the temple of the appropriate god and offer them a gift.

Temples were often beautifully decorated with noble statues and colourful scenes carved on flat stone. Just as these sculptures have inspired artists down the ages, so Greek temples and public buildings have influenced modern architects. Have a look at the public buildings in your neighbourhood and see whether any of them have columns made in these ancient Greek styles.

▼ *The ruins of the Parthenon in Athens. Dedicated to Athena, the Parthenon contained a 12 metre high statue of the goddess, made of gold and ivory.*
   Every year the Athenians held a festival in honour of Athena, which included singing, dancing, feasting, athletics and a procession to the Parthenon.

Doric

Ionic

Corinthian

You will need: cardboard • scissors • a shoebox • ruler • paint • thin card • paper • glue • sticky tape • pencil.

To score a line, carefully run the tip of your scissors along the line, using a ruler to guide you.

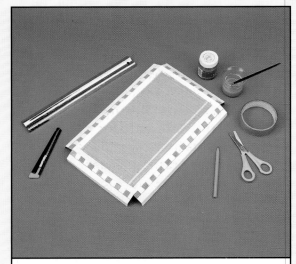

TO MAKE THE TEMPLE'S STEPS

1. Cut out several cardboard rectangles, each slightly larger than the last. (The first one needs to be a bit bigger than the shoebox). Cover each rectangle with paper, and glue them all together to make a step pyramid.

▲**3.** Draw equal-sized tabs along the longer edges of each strip. Score these lines and decorate the strips. Fold all the tabs down and tape some of them to one of the rectangles, as shown.

TO MAKE THE BASE OF THE ROOF

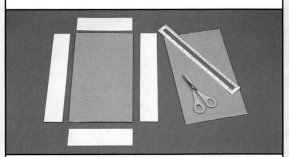

▲**2.** Cut out two more cardboard rectangles the size of your top step. Then cut out four strips of card the same length as the sides of one of the rectangles. Make sure that all four strips are the same width.

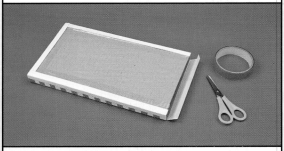

▲**4.** Tape the remaining tabs to the other rectangle, as shown.

TO MAKE THE TOP OF THE ROOF

5. Draw two triangles onto some card. The base of each triangle must be the same length as the width of the roof base. The height of each triangle should be shorter than its base.

6. Add tabs to the sides of both triangles, cut them out and decorate them. Paint the shoebox as well, to make it look like the inner part of a temple.

7. Cut out a piece of card the same length as the base of your roof. It should be twice as wide as one of the shorter sides of your triangles. Fold the card in half lengthways and glue it to the triangles to form a roof top. Glue both parts of the roof together. Stand the shoebox temple on the steps and stick its roof in place.

TO MAKE THE COLUMNS

8. Cut out a rectangle of paper, the same height as your shoebox. Then cut out a paper circle the same width as this rectangle. Paint the rectangle, roll it into a tube and glue its edges down so that they just overlap.

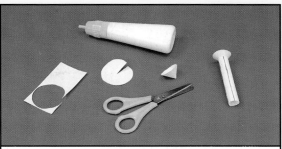

▲**9.** Snip the paper circle as shown, and roll and glue it into a cone. Trim the open end of the cone if it's uneven, and glue the cone and tube together.

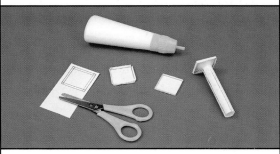

▲**10.** Make a paper box as shown, and glue it to the top of your column. The base of the box should be about the same width as the cone. Make more columns in the same way and glue them into place. You'll need to trim their bases slightly to make them fit.

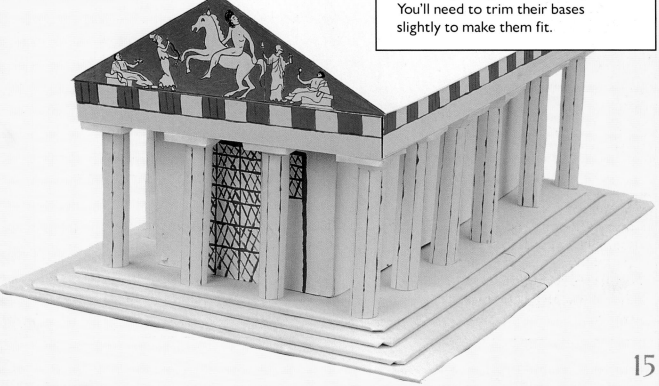

Men and Monsters

The early Greeks didn't have our knowledge of natural science. So they invented fabulous stories about their gods to explain mysteries of nature, such as how the world began and why the seasons change.

They also told thrilling tales about legendary heroes. Although some of these heroes may well have existed, their dare-devil deeds were often exaggerated to make them seem like supermen.

Perseus was one of the Greeks' favourite heroes. His adventures began when a wicked king called Polydectes sent him to find the cave of the three Gorgons and bring back the head of Medusa. This was no easy task, as Perseus well knew, for the snake-haired Medusa was so ugly that anyone who looked upon her immediately turned to stone.

Luckily for Perseus, the goddess Athena decided to help. Warning him never to look at Medusa directly, she gave him a mirror-like shield. Thus armed, Perseus put on his winged sandals and flew off to meet his foe.

When he reached Medusa's lair, Perseus quickly got to work. Holding up his shield, he stared at her reflection and, with a single blow, sliced off her head and bundled it into his bag.

But Perseus's adventures did not end there. On his way home, he turned the god Atlas into a mountain, rescued a princess from a sea monster and killed an army of men. He then strolled into Polydectes's palace and, holding up Medusa's severed head, turned the king to stone.

MEDUSA'S MASK

You will need: thin card • ruler • scissors • craft knife • glue • a strip of flat elastic • stapler • felt • pipe cleaners • paper.

Ask a grown-up to help you as the craft knife will be sharp!

1. Trace the template on page 17 onto some card and cut it out. Hold the mask against your face and ask a friend to check that the eye, nose and mouth holes are in the right position before you cut them out. Don't cut the nose away completely, though. Just make a slit along the centre and base lines and open out the two flaps.

TO MAKE THE NOSE

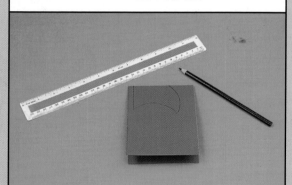

▲ **2.** Fold a piece of card in half and draw a nose on it, with the top edge along the fold. Make sure that the base of the nose is straight and slightly longer than the raised-up flaps on the mask.

3. Cut around this nose shape, except where it touches the fold, and glue its front edges together. Wait for the glue to dry and stick the nose to the outside of your mask's flaps.

If you don't like the nose shown here, draw another shape. A long pointed nose or a roof-shaped one with a card triangle at the front would work just as well.

TO MAKE THE LIPS

4. Cut out a pair of card lips, and stick them to the corners of your mask's mouth so that they stand out. Make other features, such as eyelids, in the same way.

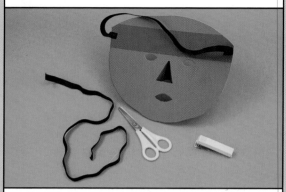

▲ **5.** To strengthen the forehead, glue a band of card onto the back of the mask, just above the eye holes. Staple a strip of elastic to the ends of this band.

TO MAKE THE HAIR

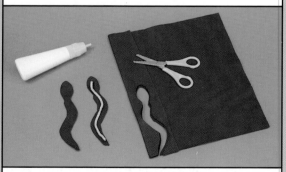

▲ **6.** Fold a piece of felt in half, draw a snake and cut it out. Bend a pipe cleaner so that it follows the curve of your snake and glue it between both pieces of felt.

7. Make as many snakes as you need. Decorate them with card or felt, glue them to your mask and get set to petrify your friends!

Here are some other snake making methods you could try.

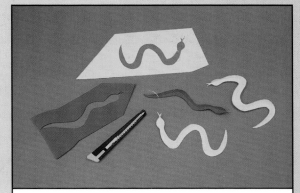

▲ **8.** Hold a paper snake in one hand, and with the other, pull a pair of *closed* scissors along the underside of the paper, as shown. Do this for a short distance, and then turn the snake over and curl another bit. Keep doing this until your snake is swirly.

▲ **9.** To make less "ripply" snakes, cut a snake out of thin card and score a curve down the centre of its body.

SCHOOLS AND SCHOLARS

When he was about seven years old, a citizen's son was sent to school where he was taught everything he needed to know to become a good citizen. Poetry, music and manners were as much a part of his education as reading, writing and arithmetic. Physical training was considered important, too, because every state needed strong, agile citizens to serve in its army.

WAX SCRATCHING
Greek schoolboys had neither pens, paper or rubbers. Each pupil wrote on a wax-coated wooden tablet, using a stick sharpened at one end. The other end of the stick was used for rubbing out mistakes.

CAPITAL LETTER	SMALL LETTER	LETTER NAME	English Sound
A	α	ALPHA	a
B	β	BETA	b
Γ	γ	GAMMA	g
Δ	δ	DELTA	d
E	ε	EPSILON	e
Z	ʒ	ZETA	z
H	η	ETA	e or ay
Θ	θ	THETA	th
I	ι	IOTA	i
K	κ	KAPPA	k
Λ	λ	LAMBDA	l
M	μ	MU	m
N	ν	NU	n
Ξ	ξ	XI	x or ks
O	ο	OMICRON	o
Π	π	PI	p
P	ρ	RHO	r
Σ	ς s	SIGMA	s
T	τ	TAU	t
Y	υ	UPSILON	u or oo
Φ	φ	PHI	f or ph
X	χ	CHI	ch
Ψ	ψ	PSI	ps
Ω	ω	OMEGA	oh

▲ A school lesson in progress. Privileged boys were often accompanied to school by a slave called a paidagogos. The bearded man in this picture is probably a paidagogos. He was supposed to keep an eye on his young master and make sure that he behaved himself.

▲ This is the Greek alphabet. The letters in black show how each Greek letter sounds in English.

If you made the vase on page 8, you could sign your name on it in Greek, just as ancient potters and artists used to do. If your name needs a letter not shown here, use a letter with a similar sound instead. For example you can use **K** for c or q, **φ** for v and **ou** for w. **c** written over a letter means that the letter should be pronounced with an h. S at the end of a word is written **S** not **ς**

Although girls often learned to read and write, they didn't go to school. Instead they had to stay at home with their mothers, who taught them domestic skills.

SENIOR STUDIES

Unlike poor boys who often couldn't afford a full education, wealthy youths usually left school at about 15. Those who wanted to continue their studies went along to their local gymnasium, or sports centre, to listen to the teachings of wise men called philosophers. In the 300s BC, permanent schools were set up at gymnasiums in Athens, where young men could go to discuss science, maths, politics and human nature.

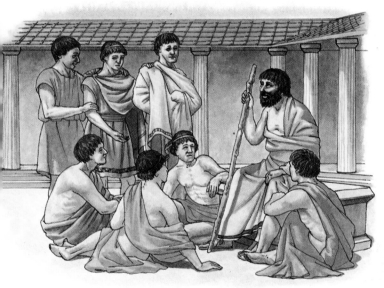

Greek philosophers challenged traditional ideas about the world in which they lived. Instead of explaining everything in religious terms, they looked for other explanations. Thanks to these men, great scientific discoveries were made possible. We still use some of their ideas today.

COUNTING FRAMES

Greek schoolboys did their sums on a wooden frame with rows of beads on it. This was called an abacus. Each of the beads on the top row was worth one unit, those on the middle row were worth 10, and those on the bottom row were each worth 100.

You will need: 3 blocks of balsa wood (preferably the same size) • 3 balsa dowels • balsa cement • air hardening modelling clay • acrylic paint.

1. Roll some modelling clay into 27 little balls. Skewer each ball with a dowel, and leave them somewhere warm to dry.

2. When your beads have dried, paint them. Let the paint dry thoroughly and slide nine beads onto each dowel.

3. Glue the three blocks of balsa wood together, as shown. Then glue each of the dowels into place and start counting!

FUN AND GAMES

Like most people, the ancient Greeks enjoyed playing games. Typical games of that time included a board game similar to backgammon, a team game similar to hockey, and a party game called cottabos, which involved flicking the remains of a cup of wine at some unsuspecting target!

Astragali, or knucklebones, was also popular. This game was a bit like jacks. Using one hand only, each player threw five small animal bones into the air and tried to catch them on the back of their hand. If they dropped any bones, they had to pick them up without losing those already on the back of their hand. This could be very tricky as you'll discover if try playing knucklebones using small pebbles!

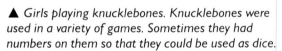

▲ *Girls playing knucklebones. Knucklebones were used in a variety of games. Sometimes they had numbers on them so that they could be used as dice.*

TOYS FOR BOYS AND GIRLS

Wealthy children were often given toys to play with – rolling hoops and sticks, clay balls and tops, and dolls made of leather, clay or beeswax.

A Greek doll was a bit like a puppet. Its body, arms and legs were made separately and then strung together. Look at the picture shown here, and try to make your own Greek doll, using air hardening modelling clay and string.

22

MAKING MUSIC

Although we don't know what ancient Greek music sounded like, we do know that there was plenty of it! Births, marriages, love and drinking were all celebrated in song. Poetry was often recited to music as well, and pipe players were used to keep rowers or marching soldiers in time with each other.

As vase paintings show, the Greeks played many different instruments including cymbals, drums, pan-pipes, lyres and auloi (double pipes).

The pan-pipes were named after Pan, the god of nature. Unlike the Olympians, Pan was half-goat. According to legend, a nymph called Syrinx was so anxious to escape his unwanted advances that she turned herself into a reed. Unable to find her, Pan cut several reeds and turned them into pan-pipes, or syrinx.

PIPE PLAYING

You will need: eight plastic drinking straws (the widest you can find) • glue • scissors • ruler • a strip of card about 6cm by 25cm • coloured pencils.

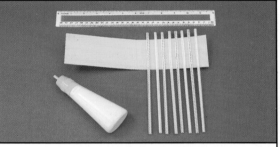

▲ **I.** Decorate one side of the card and then glue the straws, 1¼ cm apart, onto the undecorated side. Make sure that the top of the straws are in line.

2. Fold and glue the remaining card across the straws and then cut the longer ends so that each straw is slightly shorter than the one before.

3. To play your pipes, point the straws downwards and blow gently across the top of them.

23

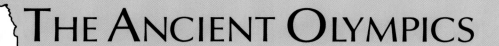

THE ANCIENT OLYMPICS

Every fourth summer, hundreds of Greeks stopped whatever they were doing and set off for Olympia, to attend the Olympic Games.

The Olympics were the most important of all the Greek games. Before they began, heralds travelled through Greece and the colonies, announcing that all inter-state wars had to stop so that everyone could visit Olympia in safety. Everyone, that is, except married women! Wives were not allowed to attend the Games and girls and slaves were forbidden to compete. Women had their own games, held every four years in honour of Hera.

Like all major sports contests, the Olympic Games were part of a religious festival. Olympia was sacred to Zeus, and athletes competed in his honour.

DAY ONE
The first day of the Games was devoted to boys' wrestling, running and boxing events, as well as trumpeters' competitions and poetry recitals.

DAY TWO
The second day of the Games was probably the most spectacular. Jockeys raced barebacked, and charioteers charged round and round two posts at either end of a track. Chariot races were filled with thrills and spills. With sometimes as many as 40 chariots skidding and thundering down the dusty track, it's not surprising that few starters finished the course.

The Pentathlon was also held on the second day. This event, which consisted of wrestling, running, jumping, discus and javelin throwing, was very popular. The Greeks didn't admire specialists. They preferred citizens who were good all-rounders.

DAY THREE
The third day was given over to running races and a procession to the temple of Zeus. There, 100 oxen were sacrificed and some of the meat was eaten at a feast.

DAY FOUR

The real crowd pullers, wrestling and boxing, were held on the fourth day. Boxing was a very straightforward event. Each boxer simply bound his fists with leather strips and then hit his opponent as hard as he could until one of them either collapsed or gave up!

Running races were also held on the fourth day, but unlike the earlier races, athletes had to sprint in their armour.

DAY FIVE

The final day of the Games was devoted to prize giving. Apart from the personal glory of winning, victors were presented with palm branches, olive wreaths and wool ribbons. They were also treated to a huge banquet.

The Ancient Olympics started in about 776 BC and came to an end in AD 395, when Olympia was buried by two earthquakes. The first modern Olympic Games started in 1896.

25

A Day At The Theatre

The first Greek plays were song and dance shows performed by a Chorus of men, in honour of Dionysos, the god of wine. Later on, an actor was introduced who talked to the Chorus, and during the Classical Period, a second and third actor were added. From these beginnings, plays, as we know them, developed.

KINGS AND CLOWNS

Ancient Greek plays were not performed every night. They were put on as part of annual religious festivals, and prizes were awarded for the best tragedy and the best comedy.

Writers of tragedy usually based their plays on well-known stories about long gone heroes and kings. They then altered or developed the story to express their own ideas about life or man's struggle with the gods.

Unlike tragedies which were passionate and sad, comedies were riotously rude with plenty of slapstick humour. Comic writers used their plays to comment upon the times in which they lived and to poke fun at famous people. The great comic playwright, Aristophanes, was often so outrageously rude that had he lived today, he would probably have spent most of his time in a law court, being sued!

▼ *Greek theatres were built in a semi-circle, usually on a hillside. The building at the back of the circular stage was called the skene. It contained the actors' dressing rooms and was often painted to look like scenery.*

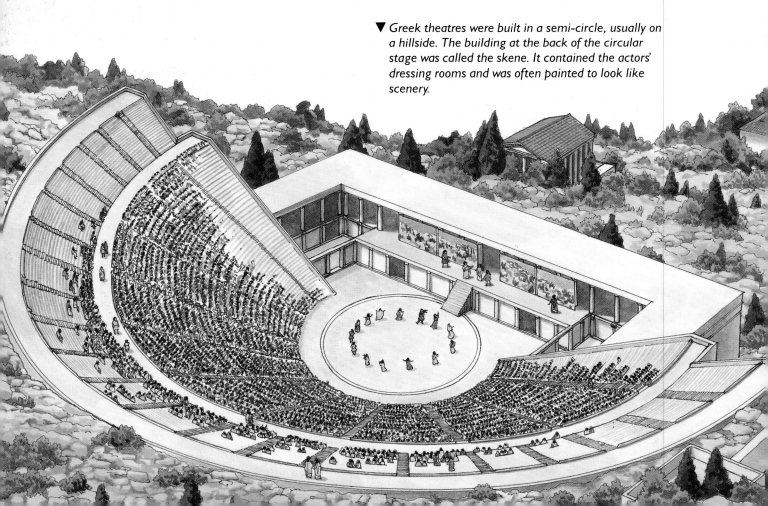

GROUP OUTINGS

Going to the theatre was a great social event. Thousands of people would take a packed lunch and spend the whole day watching several plays in a row. Even those who couldn't afford a ticket were encouraged to attend. Their entrance fees were paid for by the State.

MASKED MEN

Greek theatres were huge. Many of them could seat at least 18,000 people. To help those at the back to hear what was going on, actors wore large, open-mouthed masks, which projected their voices. The expressions on these exaggerated masks also showed what type of character the actor was playing.

   Mask wearing was useful in other ways, too. With often only three actors to play all the main parts, mask swapping

▲ *The plays of the ancient Greeks are still performed today. Sometimes they are even performed in the very theatres they first appeared in, over 2,000 years ago.*

was a quick and easy way for an actor to change character. Also, as all Greek actors were men, feminine-looking masks helped them to play female characters.

27

THE END OF CLASSICAL GREECE

By the end of the Classical Period, most Greek states were so exhausted by their frequent wars with each other that they were powerless against an outside invader, Macedonia. In 338 BC, Philip II of Macedonia seized control of Greece, but his rule was short-lived. In 336 BC he was assassinated, and his son, Alexander the Great, succeeded him.

Like his father, Alexander was a military genius. Under his leadership, the Greek and Macedonian armies conquered a vast empire which stretched from the Mediterranean Sea to the Indian Ocean. As a result, Greek customs, ideas and language were spread across the ancient world.

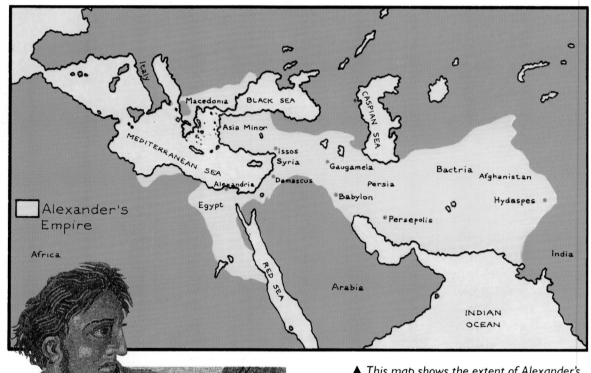

▲ This map shows the extent of Alexander's empire. The picture of him comes from a Roman mosaic.

THE CITY OF LEARNING
Wherever he went, Alexander founded cities, the greatest of which was Alexandria on the north coast of Egypt. This thriving new city soon became the intellectual capital of the Greek world, and scholars working there made astounding new discoveries.

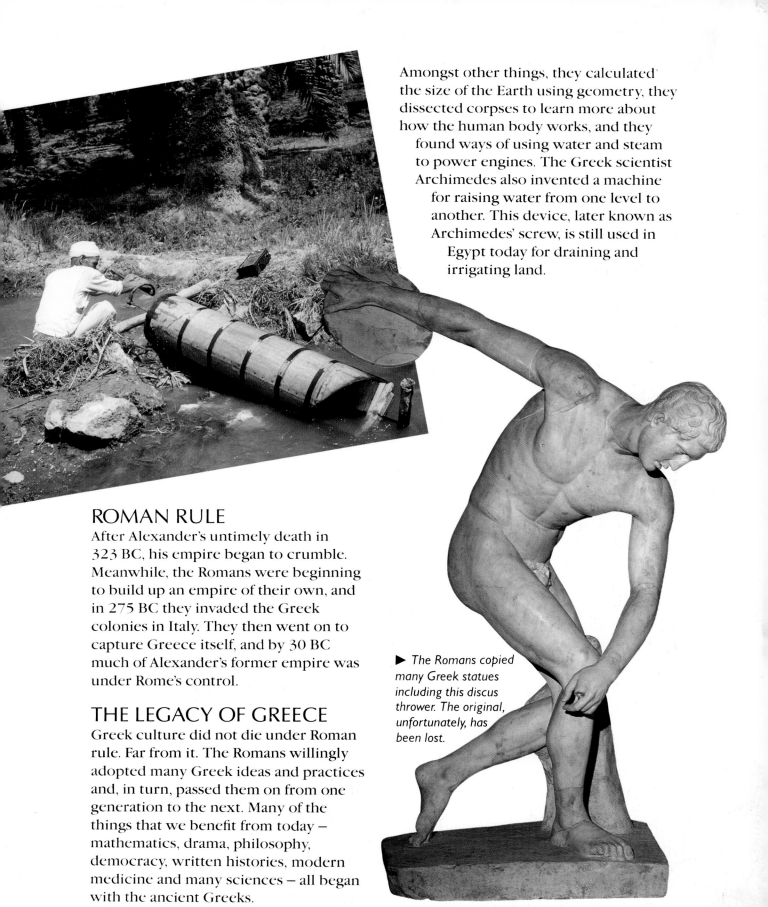

Amongst other things, they calculated the size of the Earth using geometry, they dissected corpses to learn more about how the human body works, and they found ways of using water and steam to power engines. The Greek scientist Archimedes also invented a machine for raising water from one level to another. This device, later known as Archimedes' screw, is still used in Egypt today for draining and irrigating land.

ROMAN RULE

After Alexander's untimely death in 323 BC, his empire began to crumble. Meanwhile, the Romans were beginning to build up an empire of their own, and in 275 BC they invaded the Greek colonies in Italy. They then went on to capture Greece itself, and by 30 BC much of Alexander's former empire was under Rome's control.

THE LEGACY OF GREECE

Greek culture did not die under Roman rule. Far from it. The Romans willingly adopted many Greek ideas and practices and, in turn, passed them on from one generation to the next. Many of the things that we benefit from today – mathematics, drama, philosophy, democracy, written histories, modern medicine and many sciences – all began with the ancient Greeks.

▶ *The Romans copied many Greek statues including this discus thrower. The original, unfortunately, has been lost.*

GLOSSARY

Brazier – a portable metal stand used for burning charcoal.

Chorus – a group of players who, speaking in unison, commented upon the action of a play. The Chorus sometimes danced and sang as well.

Corinthian – a style of architecture, named after the city of Corinth. Corinthian columns were very popular with the Romans.

Democracy – a system of government in which all citizens have a say in how their state or country is run. The word "democracy" comes from the Greek words "demos" (people) and "kratia" (power).

Doric – a style of architecture, named after a tribe of people called Dorians, who became powerful in Greece after the collapse of the Mycenaean civilization. Doric columns were popular on mainland Greece.

Gorgon – one of three female winged monsters with snakes for hair, who turned men to stone with their gaze.

Grecian – Greek

Ionic – a style of architecture, named after Ionia. Ionic columns were most popular in the eastern Greek colonies and on the islands.

Kiln – a large oven used for baking, or firing, pottery. There was usually a hole in the door of the kiln so that the potter could see what was happening inside.

Legacy – a gift inherited from a dead person or persons.

Lot – choosing an official by lot was similar to picking his name out of a hat.

Lyre – a stringed musical instrument, a bit like a small harp. Early Greek lyres were made from the horns of an ox and the shell of a tortoise. According to the Greek myths, the lyre was invented by the god Hermes.

Nymph – a minor goddess of nature.

Petrify, to – to turn to stone or to freeze in horror.

Philosopher – a lover of wisdom. The first philosophers studied practically everything in the world around them – nature, plants, rocks, animals, people etc. Today, philosophers study the nature of human behaviour and ask questions about the meaning of life.

Sacrifice – a gift, usually a slaughtered animal, offered on an altar to a god in ancient times.

Slip – a paste made from clay and water. The ancient Greeks made slip black by adding wood ash to it.

Tyrant – a ruler with unrestricted power. We use the word today to mean a cruel, overpowering bully.

RESOURCES

PLACES TO VISIT

Here is a list of some of the museums where you can see ancient Greek artefacts. Ask your local tourist information centre for advice on local museums with collections of ancient Greek objects.

Ashmolean Museum

Beaumont Street
Oxford
OX1 2PH
There is a large collection of ancient Greek pottery held at this museum.

British Museum

Great Russell Street
London
WC1B 3DG
The British Museum has several rooms crammed with ancient Greek artefacts.

The Shefton Museum of Greek Art and Archaeology

Department of Classics
Armstrong Building
The Quadrangle
Newcastle University
Newcastle upon Tyne
NE1 7RU
This museum has a collection of ancient Greek artefacts and welcomes school visits.

The Ure Museum of Greek Archaeology

Department of Classics
University of Reading
Whiteknights
Reading
RG6 6AA
Visit this museum to see its large collection of ancient Greek pottery and other everyday objects from that time.

USEFUL WEBSITES

www.ancientgreece.co.uk/menu.html
A British Museum website that covers many aspects of life in ancient Greece. Includes photographs of artefacts, maps, information and challenges.

www.arwhead.com/Greeks
Lots of information about ancient Greece.

www.bbc.co.uk/schools/ancientgreece/main_menu.shtml
Learn about life in ancient Greece, explore on-line resources or read a cartoon story.

www.mythweb.com/heroes/heroes.html
Read the stories of some ancient Greek heroes, illustrated with cartoons.

www.thebritishmuseum.ac.uk/explore/families_and_children.aspx
Click on 'Sport in ancient Greece' for fascinating information and photographs of objects relating to the Olympic Games and other sporting events in ancient Greece.

http://home.freeuk.net/elloughton13/gcontent.htm
Snaith Primary School's site about ancient Greece explores life in Athens and Sparta.

Note to parents and teachers: Every effort has been made by the Publishers to ensure that these websites are suitable for children, that they are of the highest educational value, and that they contain no inappropriate or offensive material. However, because of the nature of the Internet, it is impossible to guarantee that the contents of these sites will not be altered. We strongly advise that Internet access is supervised by a responsible adult.

INDEX

Additional photographs: Ancient Art & Architecture Collection 7(t), 13(b), 22(m), 23(l), 28(b), 29(both); reproduced by courtesy of the British Museum 22(m); Mansell Collection 20(bl); Peter Clayton 22(t); Zefa 27(t).